PICTURING JESUS

Picturing Jesus

Simon Jones

with illustrations by Taffy

Series Editor: James Jones

the bible reading fellowship
OPENING THE BIBLE

Text copyright Simon Jones © 1993
Illustrations copyright Taffy © 1993

The author asserts the moral right
to be identified as the author of this work

Published by
The Bible Reading Fellowship
Peter's Way
Sandy Lane West
Oxford
OX4 5HG
ISBN 0 7459 2571 5
Albatross Books Pty Ltd
PO Box 320
Sutherland
NSW 2232
Australia
ISBN 0 7324 0768 0

First edition 1993
All rights reserved

Acknowledgments

Scriptures quoted from the Good News Bible published by The Bible Societies/HarperCollins Publishers Ltd., UK © American Bible Society, 1966, 1971, 1976, 1992, with permission.

A catalogue record for this book is available from the British Library

Printed and bound in Malta

Contents

1	Bread role	15	Knowing me, knowing you!
2	Oi you!!	16	The body beautiful!
3	Hungry?	17	I am the resurrection
4	Thirsty?	18	What does it matter? (1)
5	Brilliant!	19	What does it matter? (2)
6	Life light	20	Before and after
7	It's a dark world out there!	21	100% proof
8	Shiney people	22	The way
9	I am the gate	23	The truth, the whole truth . . .
10	The rescue plan	24	Source of life!
11	Fear	25	Good news to gossip!
12	Filled with life!	26	I am the real vine!
13	Good one!	27	United!!
14	Why die?	28	Branching out!

1

What's your favourite meal from the list below? (tick one)

☐ Fish and chips
☐ Pizza
☐ Curry
☐ Roast chicken
☐ Steak
☐ Hamburger
☐ Other

Why is it your best meal? We enjoy our favourite meal because it satisfies our hunger and tingles our taste-buds—it tastes good!

Moses led the Jewish people out of slavery in Egypt towards the land God had promised them. During the journey they ran out of food. They had nothing to satisfy their hunger or tingle their tast-buds! So God sent them Manna from heaven. Manna was pieces of bread that tasted like biscuits and honey (see Exodus chapter 16)

BREAD ROLE

1

In Jesus' day, bread was a vital part of their diet—without it they died. They didn't have the choice of food that we see when we walk into a supermarket! Bread gave their bodies life and strength. Jesus is the bread of life. He is the only one who can give us life and strength. Not just to our bodies (that's the outside of us), but to our spirit (that's the inside of us). Without Jesus, the inside bit of us dies! With Jesus, we come alive!

 The people one day asked Jesus whether he could do a Manna bread miracle like Moses to prove that he was from God. Jesus said to them...

'I am telling you the truth... What Moses gave you was not the bread from heaven; it is my Father who gives you the real bread from heaven. For the bread that God gives is he who comes down from heaven and gives life to the world.' 'Sir,' they asked him, 'give us this bread always.' 'I am the bread of life,' Jesus told them.

John 6:32–35

Next time you're about to have something to eat pray this prayer:

Thank you Lord Jesus for this food that keeps me alive on the outside. Thank you for your friendship that keeps my spirit alive. Amen.

2

Oi you!!

You see a friend on the other side of the road, what words would you use to grab their attention? (tick one)

☐ 'Oi!'
☐ 'Hey!'
☐ 'Wotcha!'
☐ 'Dave!' (their name)
☐ 'Alright!'
☐ 'Oi ugly!'
☐ Other

Now what do you say to call them over (tick one)

☐ 'Come here'
☐ 'Fancy a coke?'
☐ 'Let's do lunch'
☐ 'Wait there'
☐ 'Hang on a minute'
☐ Wave madly at them

I was walking along the road with my friend Rob. I was talking to him but he was looking the other way, at an old girlfriend who was walking on the other side. This went on for a few minutes until I shouted, 'Rob watch out!' He was still ignoring me as he walked slap bang into the lampost!

Jesus said to the people, 'come to me...' He left the decision to come or not up to them. I was upset that my friend Rob hadn't listened to me. I could have saved him losing his two front teeth. We like to have people listen to us. It's bad news when someone ignores you completely! If it upsets us, imagine how much it upsets God when people don't listen to him. Jesus was God's greatest spokesman.

Oi! LOOK OUT!!

Jesus said:

'I am the bread of life... He who comes to me will never be hungry.'

John 6:35

2

God has grabbed our attention by sending Jesus. And yet when he invited people to come to him, he never forced them. When Jesus says, 'come to me...', we musn't look the other way and pretend not to hear! Just like I kept talking to my friend Rob, so Jesus keeps talking to us. We have to keep listening and doing what he says. Building a friendship is as much listening as it is speaking. The same is true of our friendship with Jesus.

There are lots of ways you can practice listening to Jesus. Tick the ones you'll try today.

- ☐ 1 Read a verse from John's Gospel (such as John 6:35) then be quiet and pray, 'Lord, what are you saying to me from this verse?'
- ☐ 2 When you need guidance about something at school or work, stop and pray, 'Lord what do *you* want me to do?'
- ☐ 3 Before a sermon or talk at church, ask God to speak to you.
- ☐ 4 At the end of the day, write down what's been on your mind. Pray and see if God has been putting some of it there.

Open our ears Lord—we want to hear Jesus. Show us how we can be better listeners to him. In Jesus' name. Amen.

3

> *'I am the bread of life,'* Jesus told them. *'He who comes to me will never be hungry.'*
>
> John 6:35

Did Jesus mean that when we become Christians, we won't need to eat ever again? In a way, yes!

God made people with a built-in need for him. Only Jesus meets that need. A baby has a built-in need for milk. If you give that baby a pint of beer they'll be very sick! So, when people search for God, the searching should begin and end with Jesus. Anything else will be about as good as beer to a baby! Some try and satisfy their need for God in different ways. On the chart below put a **J** by the things that Jesus would want you to do.

Read horoscopes	_____
Meditate	_____
Go to church	_____
Consult fortune teller	_____
Practice yoga	_____
Pray	_____
Dabble in drugs	_____
Read the Bible	_____
Play with ouija board	_____
Use tarot cards	_____

Jesus said that *he* was the way to have our hunger for God satisfied. We don't need to try other ways!

A friend of mine took a tin of dog food into a school. He opened it in front of his mates and began eating the contents. The response was obvious—'yuk!' What they didn't know was that he'd opened the tin the night

before. Having cleaned out all the dog food, he replaced it with chocolate and gelatine, leaving it overnight in the fridge to harden up. All he then had to do when faced with his friends was open it the other end!

Many people take one look at the Christian faith and think, 'yuk, this Jesus business is nonsense!' without ever taking a closer look at all that's inside!

King David said in one of his psalms:

Taste and see that the Lord is good.
Psalm 34:8 (NIV)

When we truly come to Jesus and ask him to be in our lives, we don't need to look in other places to find God. We've tasted and seen that Jesus is the best.

When a friend next says to you, 'Why do you go to church?' or 'Why do you read the Bible?' or 'Why bother with that youth group?' you could think of King David's words and say, 'Why not come with me and see for yourself!'

Almighty God, thank you that Jesus satisfies our inner hunger for you. Help us to do all our spiritual searching through him. Amen.

4

> *'I am the bread of life,'* Jesus told them. *'He who comes to me will never be hungry; he who believes in me will never be thirsty.'*
> John 6:35

Shade in the bottle you would drink.

Imagine you've walked fifty miles into the Sahara desert. You reach for your water bottle only to find that you forgot it! The temperature is 120 degrees in the shade. The sun burns your back... your mouth dries up... you're feeling dizzy. Then you see it, a small oasis ahead of you. As you reach the small cluster of palm trees you see two bottles placed on a rock. One is an ice-chilled bottle of coke, the other, a plain old bottle of water. Which is going to quench your thirst and help you to carry on?

Coke may look better, but five minutes after drinking it, the sugary liquid will make you thirsty again. Water reaches the parts other drinks simply cannot reach! It's a longer-lasting thirst quencher!

4

 Jesus was talking to a woman by a well one day and he pointed at the water and said:

 Read 2 Corinthians 5:5

'Whoever drinks this water will be thirst again, but whoever drinks the water that I will give him will never be thirsty again. The water I give him will become in him a spring which will provide him with life-giving water and give him eternal life.'

John 4:13–14

God is the one who has prepared us for this change, and he gave us his Spirit as the guarantee of all that he has in store for us.

Almighty God, fill me with your life-giving Spirit. I praise you that your Holy Spirit never runs out in me!
Amen.

The person at the oasis will never have their thirst quenched until they take the bottle of water and drink from it. When we reach out to Jesus and believe in him, he reaches out to us and gives us his life-giving Holy Spirit to be in us. This means that God becomes our closest friend. We begin to learn what he wants for our lives. Others will see how he changes us, makes us more like Jesus. God provides us with his life-giving water—a spring that never runs out even after we die!

5

In this setting Jesus spoke up and said:

▎ *'I am the light of the world . . .'*
John 8:12

BRILLIANT

Jesus was in Jerusalem, capital city of Israel. He'd gone there for a big Jewish celebration called, 'the Feast of the Tabernacles' (the Jews lived in tabernacles or tents during their escape from Egypt—this feast helped them remember that time). It was like a bank holiday, and people were packed into the city. The temple was where the Jews came to worship God. On the inside of the temple was a place to give money for the poor. Most people came there to give small gifts of cash! Jesus stood here to teach all the passers by. As darkness fell on the first night of the feast, hundreds of candles were lit and lifted high into the sky. There were *so* many candles that most of the city was lit up.

If it's dark while you're reading this, switch out all the lights in your room and wait a few seconds. Then switch them back on.

Write down how it felt to be in darkness.

....

....

....

5

Notice when the lights are on that there's enough light for the whole room. The darkness doesn't bunch up in one corner, it's pushed out by the light. Darkness can be pretty scary. There's a story of a prisoner in the Second World War who was locked in a dark room for several days. He lost all sense of time and forgot what light was like. The darkness brought fear, uncertainty, blindness, feeling lost. It was a shock when he was allowed to have some light, but after a while he knew the darkness was gone. Things returned back to normal. Jesus said that he was the light for the *whole* world. Jesus wants everyone's life to return back to normal. He wants to push out fear, uncertainty, a feeling of lostness, despair. Some say that Jesus is only relevant for certain people. But Jesus told us that he came to be a light for *everyone* ... black people, white people, rich, poor, old, young, you, me and everyone.

Let's pray that more people switch on to the light of Jesus! In the prayer below put the name of a person who you think will never switch on to Jesus.

Lord, I'm sorry I forget that you want to shine your light into every person's life. I pray for .... that he/she will turn and see the light of your love. Amen.

6

I once went caving with five friends. The only equipment we had were tin hats and candles. Halfway down a narrow tunnel called 'the drainpipe' I sneezed and blew out my candle. The only thing that broke through the darkness was the sound of my friends up ahead. I followed the sound of their shouts and crept slowly out of the darkness into the light.

Jesus said . . .

'*I am the light of the world . . . Whoever follows me will have the light of life . . .*'

John 8:12

We all follow somebody at some time.

If each of these people called, 'Follow me,' who would you go with? (Tick one)

- ☐ Politician
- ☐ Vicar
- ☐ Best friend
- ☐ Favourite group
- ☐ Boyfriend/Girlfriend
- ☐ Parents
- ☐ Film star
- ☐ Youth Leader
- ☐ Teacher
- ☐ Sporting hero

Write down what you think they could offer you in life.

....

....

....

....

Which of these words best describe what Jesus offers us?

- ☐ Fulfilment
- ☐ Happiness
- ☐ Eternal life

- ☐ A new start
- ☐ No problems
- ☐ Guidance
- ☐ Exam passes
- ☐ Purpose
- ☐ Money
- ☐ A future
- ☐ Himself

As we follow Jesus, he promises to be the light in our life. Life may not always be easy, but Jesus wants to be your light. We sometimes get worried how our friends behave or the things they say and whether we should join in. Ask Jesus to shine his light into your situation to show you the right way to react. When everyone else is swearing or pulling someone to pieces, ask Jesus to shine through you, to give you courage not to do the same.

Life light

Lord, my life is rough sometimes. But thanks, as I follow you, you light up the way ahead.

7
It's a dark world out there!

If it's night time, turn the lights out in your room. Or, find a dark room somewhere. See how long it takes for your eyes to get used to the darkness.

How long did it take before you could see objects through the darkness?

> 'I am the light of the world... Whoever follows me will have the light of life and will never walk in darkness.'
>
> John 8:12

The world can seem a pretty dark place sometimes. Jesus said that people actually *prefer* darkness to light because it's easier to do wrong things than right things. In the opening exercise, your eyes got used to the darkness. We can easily become used to the darkness in the world that we live.

Put a **D** beside the things you would say are dark:

Violence	_____
Lying	_____
Love	_____
Swearing	_____
Anger	_____
The devil	_____
Alcohol	_____
Drugs	_____
Corruption	_____
Selfishness	_____
Sleeping around	_____
Risking your life for a friend	_____

7

The devil is called the prince of darkness. His job is to stop people getting near Jesus. This way people stay in the darkness. When we begin to follow Jesus we step out of the darkness into the light. We'll never walk in darkness again! But we will have to do our bit to fight against some of the things marked in the box.

Lighten the darkness, Lord I pray. And in your mercy defend me from evil. Give me courage to be a bright light for you in all situations. Amen.

8

Here are some words from a song that I'd like you to think about:

> What would Jesus say,
> what would Jesus do,
> where would Jesus go,
> we've got to go there too . . .
> Brothers and sisters,
> we've got his work to do!

Jesus didn't just talk about himself being a light. We get a mention as lights as well!

Read Matthew 5:14–16

You are like light for the whole world. A city built on a hill cannot be hidden. No one lights a lamp and puts it under a bowl; instead he puts it on the lampstand, where it gives light for everyone in the house. In the same way your light must shine before people, so that they will see the good things you do and praise your Father in heaven.

We *musn't* ever get used to the darkness that surrounds us. We have to speak out against the wrong things that people do to each other. Also, to take action against the evil in society. This is the work Jesus did, and he's given us the job of carrying it on.

In what *practical* way could you, maybe with some friends, make a stand against the wrongs in your area? Make a list of wrong things in the left hand box, and write what action you could take in the box opposite.

Shiney

8

Wrong things	Action to take

people

Lord Jesus, thanks for lighting up my life. Help me to take a stand against the evil in my area. Show me what action I can take to be a light for you.
Amen.

9
I am the gate

 *Jesus said to his listeners:*

> '*I am telling you the truth: I am the gate for the sheep. All others who came before me are thieves and robbers, but the sheep did not listen to them.*'

John 10:7–8

When I was at school, myself and a group of mates went on a night hike in the countryside. At about 10.30pm it was pitch black and we found ourselves in the middle of a field. Which way should we go next? Then somebody spotted some large shapes moving towards us. We didn't know if they were friendly cows or mad bulls... so we ran for it! As we got near the edge of the field I spotted a gate, with a smooth field beyond. I ignored it, and dived over the fence... and... splat... I was up to my neck in pigswill! I'd have been alright if I'd used the gate!

In Jesus' day being a shepherd was a really tough job. Taking care of his sheep was his life! During the day he led the sheep to fresh grass. He made sure they didn't wander off any cliffs. He fought off beasts and bandits. He held back the fast sheep and chased on the slow ones. But at night the job was only just beginning. On the hillside, the sheep-fold was an open space enclosed by a wall. There was an opening where the sheep could get in and out, but there was no gate. When the sheep had gone inside to rest, the shepherd lay down across the

entrance. He slept there the night. He was the gate.

Jesus called himself the gate. Mark a **T** against the statements below which are true. Jesus is the gate because:

He keeps people trapped.	_____
He opens the way to God.	_____
We need protecting.	_____
He keeps us from our friends.	_____
He has his back to us.	_____
He's close-by all the time.	_____

Nowadays many still claim to be the way to God. Many talk about being in a New Age when Christianity is pointless. It's as if people are trying to climb over the fence to make friends with God. But the only way is through the Gate.

 *St Paul wrote to a group of Christians in what is now Turkey and said:*

It is through Christ that all of us, Jews and Gentiles, are able to come in the one Spirit into the presence of the Father.

Ephesians 2:18

Heavenly Father, sometimes I'm confused by so many different religions. Thank you for the plain words of Jesus. He is the gate into your presence. Help me to listen only to him. Amen.

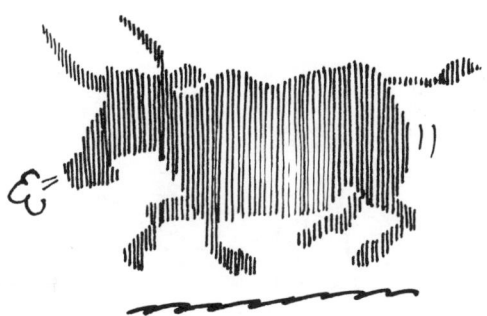

10
THE RESCUE PLAN

I was walking around our local shopping centre one day. A man came up to me holding a large floppy Bible. He put his hand out as if stopping the traffic and said three words, 'Are you saved?' It was the first time anyone had ever asked me that question. I replied, 'I dunno!' and walked off.

If someone asked you that question tommorrow, write down what you would say:

....

....

....

Jesus talked about who he was and what he'd come for:

'I am the gate. Whoever comes in by me *will be saved.*'

John 10:9

We know already that Jesus is the gate, the way in to a friendship with God. The word 'saved' means literally 'being rescued' or 'put in a safe place'. A small boy who was visiting our house got stuck in the toilet. He'd gone in, shut the door but couldn't work out how the handle worked from the inside. There was no way he could get himself out of the mess! I came along, knew he needed help, and opened the door. He ran out to safety.

10

When we believe and trust in Jesus he rescues us. We can't rescue ourselves, we need outside help. Sometimes we can feel trapped in our lives by all the rubbish that's there. Rubbish like...
Tick which things you would consider as rubbish in your life:

☐ Hatred
☐ Bad temper
☐ Lying
☐ Violence
☐ Addiction
☐ Jealousy
☐ Selfishness
☐ Bad-mouthing someone

Add your own personal 'rubbish' below:

....
....
....
....
....

Jesus says he is the gate. Not only is he the outside help we need. He's the gate who stops us being trapped in with all the rubbish! Jesus the gate is always open. We can keep coming through him with the rubbish that piles up in our life and hand it over to God.

Lord, thank you for clearing the rubbish away that's blocked me off from you. But I'm not perfect and I still need your help every day. You'll always be my Lord and my Saviour.
Amen.

11

Now be honest with yourself and write down the things you're afraid of (maybe death, or not being liked).

....

....

....

 *Jesus spoke these words to calm our fears:*

'I am the gate. Whoever comes in by me will be saved; he will come in and go out and find pasture.'

John 10:9

Some people today have 'Godophobia'. They are afraid of God. They think he dislikes us. That he's out to get us. He's the grumpy old man in the sky! People have other fears as well. Fear of being left alone, or a fear of death. Jesus said that Christians will 'come in and go out and find pasture'. This was a Jewish way of describing a life that was absolutely secure.

There are many types of fears. The word for a fear is phobia. Have a look at the fears below.

Draw a line from the fear to the correct meaning:

Fear

Acrophobia
Aerophobia
Pogonophobia
Claustrophobia
Agoraphobia
Arachnaphobia

Meaning

Fear of open spaces
Fear of spiders
Fear of enclosed spaces
Fear of heights
Fear of draughts
Fear of shaving

11

 *King David said the same thing in one of his songs:*

> The Lord will protect you from all danger; he will keep you safe. He will protect you as you come and go now and for ever.
>
> Psalm 121:7–8

We sometimes have a wrong idea about what God is like because we're looking in the wrong places. As we look at Jesus we can see what God is like. As you read through John's Gospel say to yourself as you see Jesus, 'This is God!' Once we see that our lives are in the hands of Jesus, we needn't be afraid. Our fears begin to disappear.

Think of the fear that you wrote in above, then pray...

Lord God, I get afraid sometimes. I even fear that you dislike me. Thank you that I can see you clearly in Jesus. Protect me from being afraid. Please forgive me for doubting you. It's good to know I'm in the hands of the One who loves me. Amen.

P.S. When the Bible mentions 'having the fear of the Lord' it means that we need to worship God with respect, but not to be afraid of him.

I'M TRYING TO FIND THE WORD FOR SOMEONE WHO HAS A PHOBIA OF DICTIONARIES!!!

12

Do you have friends who aren't Christians? Of course you do! Ask them what turns them off about Christianity! Make a note of their answers below.

....

....

....

....

I bet some comments went like this: 'It's old fashioned . . . boring . . . dull . . . stops you doing what you want . . . you have to give up things!'

 ***Let's recap on Jesus being the gate!***

So Jesus said again, 'I am telling you the truth: I am the gate for the sheep. All others who came before me were thieves and robbers, but the sheep did not listen to them. I am the gate. Whoever comes in by me will be saved; he will come in and go out and find pasture. The thief comes only in order to steal, kill, and destroy. I have come in order that you might have life—life in all it's fullness.

John 10:7–10

Filled with life!

12

To listen to some people you'd think that Jesus said, 'I've come to bore your life—life in all it's dullness!' Jesus offers a life that's complete. Complete forgiveness for the mistakes we've made. Complete hope in life beyond death. Complete purpose for the here and now. A vast number of opportunities to serve Jesus wherever you are.

Jesus never said it would be easy being a Christian. He will ask us to give up certain things and stop doing others. But whatever he asks you to give up, you can be sure it wasn't good for you in the first place. Jesus promised the people who follow him a full life. Boring? Never. Dull? No—full! Stops your freedom? More like, Jesus frees us! Have to give up things? Some, yes!—but gain a whole lot more!

Lord, before I knew you there was no forgiveness, no hope beyond death, no meaning to my life. It's great that you promise life in all it's fullness. I thank you for the changes that you've made to my life. Keep changing me Lord, make me more like you. Amen.

13

'I'm off for a fag!' he said, about to take a short break. I lay back in the seat staring up at the ceiling. I started to dribble, the cotton wool keeping my jaws open and the suction pump draining away the saliva! When he reappeared, he was wearing a white mask and carrying a huge needle. Then he uttered those dreaded words, 'This won't hurt!' I thought to myself, 'I hope he's a *good* dentist!'

There are certain types of people who we find it hard to trust. Mark the following people on our 'trustometer' (10 means no way, 3 means possibly).

Door-to-door salesman
0 1 2 3 4 5 6 7 8 9 10

Politician
0 1 2 3 4 5 6 7 8 9 10

Parents
0 1 2 3 4 5 6 7 8 9 10

The Church
0 1 2 3 4 5 6 7 8 9 10

Car salesman
0 1 2 3 4 5 6 7 8 9 10

Magazines
0 1 2 3 4 5 6 7 8 9 10

TV advertisers
0 1 2 3 4 5 6 7 8 9 10

Good one!

13

In Jesus' day, shepherds were dodgy characters. Most people didn't really trust them. It was a question of, 'Would you buy a used sheep off a man like this?' They had a bad reputation!

 *That's why Jesus said:*

| *'I am the good shepherd...'*
John 10:11

The good shepherd looked after the sheep. He protected them. He led them. He cared for them. When Jesus called himself the good shepherd, he didn't mean, 'I'm the efficient shepherd!' The word 'good' means more than doing a job well. It also means being reliable or excellent or kind.

You've scored types of people you find it hard to trust. Now put the word 'reliable' or 'excellent' or 'kind' in front of them. It makes a difference doesn't it!

Some of the names that God is called in the Bible may make it difficult for you to trust him! For instance, if your own father didn't treat you well, or hurt you in some way, you might find it hard to call God your 'Father in heaven'.

Or maybe it's God as Judge, or Lord, or King.

Think for a minute about the aspect(s) of God's character that you find hard. Write it in below (also in the prayer at the bottom).

....

....

....

> *Sing to the Lord, all the world! Worship the Lord with joy; come before him with happy songs! Acknowledge that the Lord is God. He made us, and we belong to him; we are his people, we are his flock. Enter the temple gates with thanksgiving, go into its courts with praise. Give thanks to him and praise him.* ***The Lord is good****; his love is eternal and his faithfulness lasts for ever.*
>
> Psalm 100

Lord, I struggle with you being .... I thank you that you are good, kind, trustworthy and excellent. Help me never to forget that God is good! Amen.

14

The bus was filled with people. The brakes had failed and it ran out of control down a steep mountain lane. As they sped down the mountain the driver saw two ways of escaping. One was to crash off the road into the valley risking certain death for all. The other was to crash through a gate into a nearby field. As he approached the field he realized that a boy was playing in front of the gate. He had to drive on, saving the passengers but killing the boy. Afterwards, the driver cried helplessly. 'Why's he crying so much?' they asked, 'he saved so many people.' 'The reason he cries,' said another, 'is because that boy was his son.'

 **Jesus said:**

> I am the good shepherd, who is willing to die for the sheep.
>
> John 10:11

Jesus did many wonderful things in his life. But all the way through his life he was telling his friends that he'd come to die. Read Mark 10:45. Like in the story above, God gave his son Jesus so that many others could be saved. But, in the bus story the boy didn't have a choice. Jesus did. He chose to do die. But why die?

 *Read Isaiah 53:5–6*

> But because of our sins he was wounded, beaten because of the evil we did. We are healed by the punishment he suffered, made whole by the blows he received. All of us were like sheep that were lost, each of us going his own way. But the Lord made the punishment fall on him, the punishment all of us deserved.

In unit 10 we talked about the rubbish in everybody's life that blocks us off from God. The Bible calls that rubbish 'sin'. Because God is completely fair he sets himself against everyone who sins, that's all of us! But because he's also completely forgiving he takes the sins away from us and onto himself. Jesus was willing to die for his sheep. But he didn't stay dead! (See unit 16.)

Why die?

14

Heavenly Father, I thank you that Jesus came to die on the cross in my place. He was completely innocent and yet he took the blame for me. Thank you Jesus. Amen.

15

Knowing me, knowing you!

What is the best way of getting to know somebody? Put a **Y** next to your best way.

Talk to them on the phone	_____
Write them a letter	_____
Chat face to face	_____
Ask them out for a meal	_____
See them when you bump into them	_____
Tell them all your secrets	_____
Say 'How about meeting up on Saturday?'	_____
Say 'I like you!'	_____
Other	_____

We saw in the last unit why Jesus the good shepherd died for his sheep. He took away the 'blockage' of sin that was between us and God.

 *But Jesus went on to say:*

> I am the good shepherd. As the Father knows me and I know the Father, in the same way I know my sheep and they know me. And I am willing to die for them.
>
> John 10:14–15

If you were unconscious and lying in a burning house, then some brave person came along and dragged you out, gave you the kiss of life and took you to hospital, you'd probably want to meet them again and say thank you! Jesus died on the cross for everyone in the world. But the benefits of what he's done become real for us when we say thank you and begin to get to know

him. Jesus knows us better than anybody else in the whole world. He even knows those secrets that we've kept from everyone else. Let's make sure we get to know him. No Jesus, no peace . . . know Jesus, know peace!

At the start of this unit we looked at ways to get to know someone. Talking, going for a meal, and so on. Place the following list in order of importance for you getting to know Jesus better:

____Prayer
____Writing down your thoughts about God each day
____Reading a Gospel
____Holy Communion
____Asking for things
____Silence
____Church on Sunday
____Praise

Lord Jesus, you know me better than anyone else. You died so that I could be free to know you. And because I know you I know the Father. Amen.

16

I want you to picture something in your mind. Ready! The Church! Write down what you saw in your mind.

....

Now put a **Yes** or **No** next to the following definitions of a Church:

A large old building	_____
A place for nice people	_____
A place for choirs	_____
A group of people who belong to Jesus	_____
A charity	_____
Jesus' body here on earth	_____
A load of sinners who say sorry to God	_____
A club	_____
Something you go to	_____

Let's see what Jesus said about the Church:

> 'There are other sheep which belong to me that are not in this sheepfold. I must bring them, too; they will listen to my voice, and they will become one flock with one shepherd.'
>
> John 10:16

Jesus says that everyone who knows him and follows him is part of his flock. That flock is his Church. In Jesus' day the people who first followed him were Jews. But as the Church grew, people from lots of different backgrounds began to follow Jesus: Greeks, Turks, Romans, Arabs and eventually you and me! So, as followers of Jesus we are linked to all the other followers of Jesus right across the world. The Bible calls

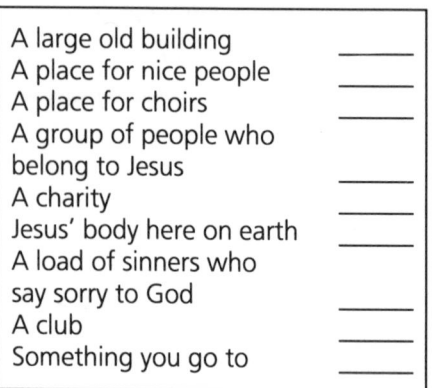

16

the Church 'a body'. This means that we all have a part to play to keep the body healthy. If we don't do our bit in the Church, then the 'body' is less healthy.

St Paul said:

> We have many parts in the one body, and all these parts have different functions. In the same way, though we are many, we are one body in union with Christ, and we are all joined to each other as different parts of one body. So we are to use our different gifts in accordance with the grace that God has given us.
>
> Romans 12:4–6

You have a part to play in your church. First you need to go to it and belong to it! Then ask yourself these questions:

What gift has God given me for the church (for example: visiting people, leading prayers, mending things)?

....

What's wrong with the church?

....

Is there anything I can do to make it better?

....

What could we do as a group (if you belong to a youth group)?

....

Who can you share your faith with, so that they too could know Jesus and be part of his flock?

....

> **P.S. Now talk to your youth leader/minister/vicar about putting these things into practice!**

Lord God, I thank you for the Church, your flock. Show me what gifts I have and how they could be used in the Church. Help me to get to know the other members of your flock in this town. Amen.

The body beautiful!

17
I am the resurrection

If you think any of the following are heroes, put an **H**. If they're superheroes put **SH**.

- Superman
- Batman
- Dick Tracey
- Spiderman
- He-Man
- Jesus
- Wonder Woman
- Sonic the Hedgehog

Fictional characters sometimes do amazing things. But only Jesus from the above list did something incredible in real life! He even told people he was going to do it!

Jesus was talking to Martha after her brother had just died.

Jesus said to her, 'I am the resurrection and the life.'

John 11:25

Even before the disciples knew that Jesus was going to be arrested, Jesus had told them that he would be killed and three days later would come back to life. It was really hard for them to believe. It can be really hard for us now to believe as well! I've heard some say, 'Jesus' resurecction can't be true because I've never experienced anyone coming back from the dead!' Make a note of your 'gut-reaction' to the resurrection.

IS IT A BIRD?....

IS IT A PLANE?...

....

....

....

It was really hard for the people who first read John's Gospel to believe in Jesus' resurrection as well. They

17

believed that when you died the body rotted and set the soul free to return to God. If the first Christians had said that just the soul of Jesus lived on and that his body was irrelevant, those first listeners could have believed more easily. So why do the Christians make it so difficult for them to believe by insisting on the bodily resurrection? The simple answer is: because it happened!!

If God is really God, would it be so difficult for him to raise Jesus back to life? Lets look at some of the Gospel facts!

> Jesus Christ is the same yesterday, today, and for ever.
>
> Hebrews 13:8

Jesus wrecked a few funerals he attended by raising the dead! Martha didn't stay sad long. Jesus brought her brother back to life. He even wrecked his own funeral!

A dead body!	Read John 19:17–37	Ask yourself: Could Jesus have survived the brutal treatment?
An empty tomb!	Read John 20:1–9	Ask yourself: Where was Jesus' body?
Many eyewitnesses!	Read John 20:10–30	Ask yourself: How many eye-witnesses?
A new community!	Read Acts 1:12–14	Ask yourself: Why pray if Jesus was dead?

Thank you Jesus, that you rose from the dead. Thank you for the evidence of the writers in the New Testament. You were really alive then and you're alive today. Amen.

NO!.... IT'S A FICTICIOUS CREATION OF AN AMERICAN PUBLISHING COMPANY...!

18
What does it matter? (1)

I sank into my comfy arm chair to 'blob-out' and watch the telly. In an instant I was glued to the TV. A famous person was chatting to an interviewer about Jesus' death and resurrection. 'I don't believe the resurrection because I don't think he really died. He simply recovered. Anyway it doesn't really matter—it's a good story!' Say after me, 'Oh yes it does matter!'

Here is one of the things people say about Jesus' death and resurrection.

The faint theory!

That Jesus never actually died on the cross, he only fainted. When he was placed in the tomb, the cool air refreshed him. He got up and left.

He'd have had to survive the beating, flogging, thorns of the trial; the nails and suffocation of the cross; the spear in his side; 36 hours in a stone tomb with no food or medical care. Then he had to have taken off the tightly wrapped linen from around him and move the stone. Finally, weak, naked, tired and hungry he'd have had to convince the disciples that he had beaten death! No, Jesus did die. The soldier at the cross saw him die. Joseph and Nicodemus took the dead body of Jesus off the cross and placed him in the tomb.

For many people the resurrection is impossible to believe. Finding out what your friends think will give you a clue as to how you can answer their problems. Do a small questionnaire with your friends. Ask them these simple questions:

1. Did Jesus die on the cross? Yes/No

2. What happened to Jesus after he was taken from the cross?

3. Do you think the resurrection of Jesus happened? Yes/No/Don't know

4. If not, what's your explanation?

18

Now pray this prayer:

Lord, help me to explain to my friends that you are alive! Amen.

19
What does it matter? (2)

Here's another of those things that people sometimes say about Jesus' resurrection!

Read what the situation would be if Jesus hadn't come alive.

Just seeing things!

That the disciples were only imagining Jesus to be alive. They had hallucinations!
But Jesus didn't just appear to one person in one place. He appeared to lots of people in lots of different places. Look up the following Bible references in the chart below and note down who he appeared to, what time he appeared and where it was.

> And if Christ has not been raised, then your faith is a delusion and you are still lost in your sins.
>
> 1 Corinthians 15:17

We believe in the resurrection not because it's a nice story, but because it's true. Also, because we experience the risen Jesus today.

	Who	What time	Where
Matthew 28:9–10			
Luke 24:1–10			
Luke 24:12			
Luke 24:13, 18, 33			
Luke 24:34			
Luke 24:36			
1 Corinthians 15:6–7			

19

Thank you Lord, all the evidence tells us that you actually came back from the dead and that many people saw you. Help me to explain to others how vital your resurrection is to the Christian faith. Amen.

20

Before and AFTER

Jesus never talked about his resurrection as an interesting subject to study! His resurrection was something to experience!

In the box below there are three people who were completely changed by Jesus' resurrection. Look up the Bible passages that show them before and after they meet the risen Jesus. Write down the words that best describe them (for example, 'happy' or 'sad').

		Before	After
Peter	(John 18:25–27) (John 21:15–17)		
Thomas	(John 20:24–25) (John 20:26–28)		
Paul	(Acts 8:3) (Acts 9:20–22)		

20

There's no doubt about it, Jesus makes a difference in people's lives. We have a friend who was deep into witchcraft. She cast spells on people. Good spells for good people, bad spells for bad people. The problem was she had no sense of good or bad! It has been a long process to see her set free from the holds of witchcraft. But, I wish you could see her now! Her face is different, she has met with Jesus. She *knows* that he's not a dead figure of the past. He is a living friend who has changed her life! Her old self has died, but her new self is a hundred times better!

Lord Jesus, you made such a difference to the lives of Peter, Thomas and Paul. Thank you that we can experience you changing us now. Make a difference in my life. Amen.

YIPEE!! HE'S ALIVE!!

P.S. If you come across someone mixed up in something like witchcraft, talk about it with a responsible adult like your youth club leader, Christian teacher, minister or priest.

21

100% PROOF

Write below what things you are a 100% certain will happen in your life.

....

....

You may have found that difficult. The only thing we can be absolutely sure of is that sooner or later our bodies will conk out! It happens to us all, presidents, prime ministers, judges, famous people, rich people, poor people, black or white, we all die!

Jesus continued to talk to Martha:

> 'I am the resurrection and the life. Whoever believes in me will live, even though he dies; and whoever lives and believes in me will never die. Do you believe this?'

John 11:25

I was listening to some people on the TV the other day. They said that by thinking the right thoughts and eating the right food they could go on living forever. Their bodies would not tire out! We'll see . . . !

21

In the space below, write a description of what eternal life is like.

....

....

....

....

....

....

Lord, I thank you that death cannot destroy our friendship. I praise you that we're friends forever. Amen.

It's hard to imagine what will happen in heaven. All we know is that there'll be no more pain or crying or sickness or anger. We'll be face to face with the Jesus who became our friend while we're on earth. Death will be a big change for us! But it won't change our friendship with Jesus. If you know Jesus now then you have an eternal friend. Jesus went through death and came out the other side alive! If you follow Jesus then you'll do the same!

22 The way

One day Jesus was telling his followers that after he'd beaten death he'd be going back to his Father in heaven:

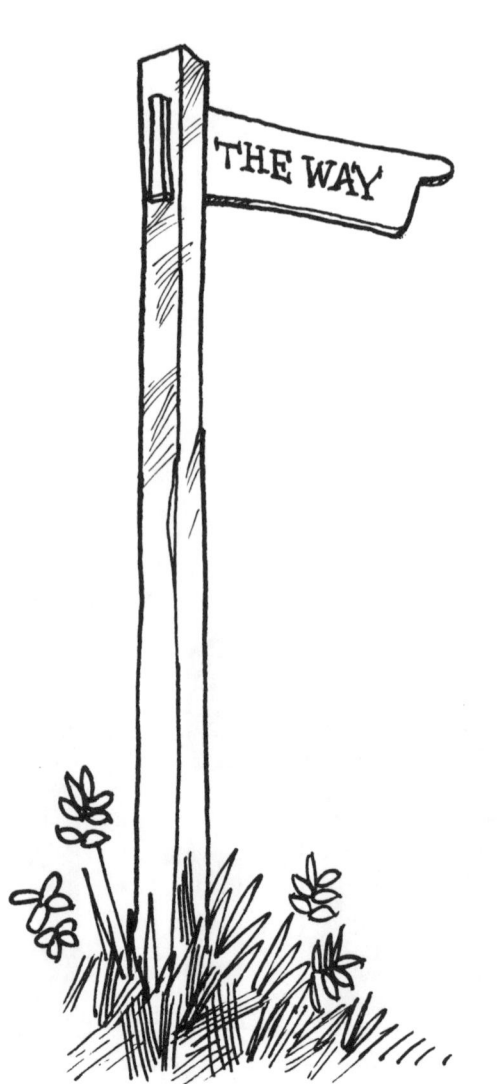

'Do not be worried and upset,' Jesus told them. *'Believe in God and believe also in me. There are many rooms in my Father's house, and I am going to prepare a place for you. I would not tell you this if it were not so. And after I go and prepare a place for you, I will come back and take you to myself, so that you will be where I am. You know the way that leads to the place where I am going.'* Thomas said to him, *'Lord, we do not know where you are going; so how can we know the way to get there?'* Jesus answered him, *'I am the way, the truth, and the life; no one goes to the Father except by me.'*

John 14:1–6

In the space below write down directions from your house to your school or your town centre.

....
....
....
....
....
....
....

22

If your directions were going to get me there, they'd have to be pretty good. Jesus gave us very accurate directions to know God as our Father. He said, 'I am the way...'

The best way for me to get to your school or town centre would be to follow you! When we follow Jesus, he brings us to our Father in heaven. Imagine what the best Father in the world would be like. Write down what he's like:

....
....
....
....
....
....
....

Our Father in heaven is a million times better than what you've written. He is the Father above all other Fathers! Now in the space on the right hand side, put this familiar prayer in your own words:

> **The Lord's Prayer shows that a good father is one who provides, forgives and protects.**

Our Father in heaven,
hallowed be your name.
Your kingdom come,
your will be done on earth as
in heaven.
Give us today our daily bread.
Forgive us our sins
as we forgive those who sin
against us.
Lead us not into temptation
but deliver us from evil.
For the kingdom, the power and
the glory are yours,
now and forever. Amen.

....
....
....
....
....
....
....
....

23 The truth, the whole truth...

We met face to face. Last time I'd got badly beaten up. This time would be different. I was ready for the fight. He stood before me. He was the leanest, meanest, roughest, toughest, rowdiest, dirtiest six-year-old in the area. As he shuffled towards me I used tactic number one, 'I'm gonna tell my daddy of you!' It failed. He kept coming, giving me that 'I couldn't care less' look. I tried emergency tactic number two, guaranteed to work with any six-year-old. 'My daddy's bigger than yours... and he's a wrestler!' He stopped, stared and then ran! I'd won, I just hoped he wouldn't find out I was lying!

Jesus claimed to *be* the truth when he said:

> 'I am the way, the truth, and the life; no one goes to the Father except by me. Now that you have known me,' he said to them, 'you will know my Father also, and from now on you do know him and you have seen him.'
>
> John 14:6–7

I lied about my father when I was six. But Jesus told us the truth about God as our Father. In fact, he did more than just *tell* us the truth. Jesus *showed* us the truth about the Father.

Read through John's Gospel and write down some words that describe what kind of person *Jesus* is in the left hand column. Then write the same word in the right hand column under the heading *Father*.

23

Jesus	Father

P.S. If someone asks you if you've ever seen God, you could say, 'I would have seen him if I'd lived when Jesus was around.'

As you look at Jesus, then you see what the Father is like. Jesus never waffled, he always spoke the truth to people... 'The Father and I are one,' he said (John 10:30).

Jesus was the truth, the whole truth, and nothing but the truth about our Father in heaven.

Thank you Jesus that you show me the truth about our Father in heaven. In this few moments of silence remind me of what my Heavenly Father is like.
(Silence for a couple of minutes.)
Thank you Lord. Amen.

24

> I am the way, the truth, and the life....
>
> John 14:6

Your parents are going away for two weeks! They leave you money for food. So what do you do? You phone all your mates the day they leave and arrange a massive rave at your place. You blow the money on things you need for the party. Loads of people turn up and the party is a blast! However, the place gets completely trashed. You don't care, you've got two weeks to clear up. There's a ring at your doorbell mid-party. You open the door and welcome the new arrivals, 'Hi... MUM, DAD!' They missed the flight and came home.

Write down what their reaction would be to the party!

....

....

....

....

Jesus told a similar story of a son who asked his father for all the cash he was owed. He left home and moved far away. He blew all the cash on wild living! But then realized that he had nothing to live on. Things got rougher and soon he decided to face his dad. He was in for a surprise.

Source of life!

24

So he got up and started back to his father. He was still a long way from home when his father saw him; his heart was filled with pity, and he ran, threw his arms round his son, and kissed him. 'Father,' the son said, 'I have sinned against God and against you. I am no longer fit to be called your son.' But the father called his servants. 'Hurry!' he said. 'Bring the best robe and put it on him. Put a ring on his finger and shoes on his feet. Then go and get the prize calf and kill it, and let us celebrate with a feast! For this son of mine was dead, but now he is alive; he was lost, but now he has been found.'

Luke 15:20–24 (whole story, verses 11–32)

The surprise in store for the son was that his father wasn't angry. Instead he showered him with love. And life began again for the son—thanks to the father's forgiveness. Like in this story, our life begins the moment we turn to the Father and say sorry. He forgives us. He wipes the slate clean. We can start again. A Christian is a forgiven sinner! Jesus brings us a new life of complete forgiveness from the Father. That's unique!

MUM, DAD,... ER...LOVELY TO SEE YOU!!

Heavenly Father, when I come to you through Jesus, you meet me with open arms to forgive me. I praise you for my forgiven life. I was lost but now I'm found! Amen.

25

Good news to gossip!

Have you heard the conversations that people have by the yoghurt section in supermarkets: 'It's the choice that I can't stand! It wouldn't be so bad if there was just one or two choices, but no, there are hundreds of choices. It's depressing really! Which shall I choose? Oh! They're all the same!' Often people say the same thing about religion: 'It's the choice I can't stand!' 'Which shall I choose?' 'They all lead to the same God anyway, don't they?'

But Jesus said:

'I am the way, the truth, and the life; no one goes to the Father except by me.'

John 14:6

In the last unit we said one of the unique things about the message of Jesus was that he brings us forgiveness. The other unique thing Jesus said was that we can only come to know God as Father through him! The word Jesus used for Father really means 'Dear Father'. God is our Dad! Some of the other religions have some of the truth about God. But it's only through Jesus that we can know God as our good Father. This is good news for every person in the world. We need to pass on this good news, especially when we hear people saying things like I heard in the supermarket.

25

1 Corinthians 15:1–11 gives a summary of the good news of the Christian message. Put it into your own words (and use pictures) as if you were explaining what Christians believe to a non-Christian friend.

....

....

....

....

Evangelism is gossipping the good news about Jesus. Put the name of a person who you could gossip the good news to below.

....

....

Now have a think about the area where you live. What kind of things go on? Could you and some Christian friends take part in a local event to broadcast the good news?

Some ideas:
▷ A float in a local carnival
▷ A Christian bookstall in a market or boot fair
▷ Zappy posters at the library
▷ Street theatre in a shopping centre (get advice with this one first!)
▷ Organise a quiz night
▷ Open air services
▷ Start a keep-fit class
▷ Form a Christian group at school—do something exciting
▷ Take a school assembly (use 'dog food' idea from unit 3)

Thank you Jesus that we can know God as our dad in heaven through you. Help us as we think of ways to gossip this good news in our neighbourhood.
Amen.

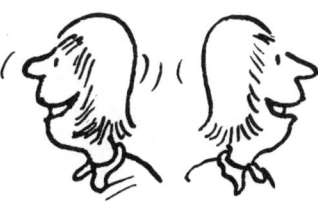

26 I am the real vine

This bush really annoyed me! It was right by our back gate. I couldn't be bothered to cut it so I let it grow. It grew and grew and grew! One day I realized that it had grown so much I couldn't even see my gate, let alone get through it! Was I a good gardener or a bad one?

Jesus gives us a clue!

> 'I am the real vine, and my Father is the gardener. He breaks off every branch in me that does not bear fruit, and he prunes every branch that does bear fruit, so that it will be clean and bear more fruit.'
>
> John 15:1–2

A good gardener prunes his bushes so that they will blossom better next time. Dead branches are removed. Good branches are pruned back. I should have pruned that bush more regularly, so that it could've grown properly.

God wants us to be 'fruity' people. To be growing more like Jesus. To be acting more like Jesus. To be speaking more like Jesus. Because of that, he wants to prune us! To get rid of the bits of our life that are no good.

vine! 26

Write on the fruit the good things you admire in other Christians:

Write on the wild branches the things that are out of control in your life:

Thank you Father that you are my gardener. You want to chop out the bits in my life that are rotten. I want to grow into the person you planned me to be. Amen.

27
United!!

I'd been trying so hard. Twelve months as a Christian and my language was improving slowly! I'd even kept my temper under control. Then it happened. My brother! As I was showing some photos to a friend, my brother was snatching them and flicking them round the room. 'Wheeeeeee!' he shouted. 'Count to ten,' I thought. 'One, two, three, fou . . . Aaaaaaah.' I hit him so hard, it hurt me! I felt so guilty. 'Some Christian,' I moaned. I've been trying so hard. Then Jesus spoke to me, 'Yes, *you've* been trying hard, why not let me have a go?'

Then the words that we're looking at today came to me:

Remain united to me, and I will remain united to you. A branch cannot bear fruit by itself; it can do so only if it remains in the vine. In the same way you cannot bear fruit unless you remain in me.

John 15:4

The only way to bear fruit as a Christian is to keep united to Jesus. Have a look at our 'united chart' below. See how you score at keeping in touch with Jesus. Be honest with yourself.

I try to read some of the Bible each day
Yes 1 2 3 4 5 6 7 8 9 Never

I feel that my prayer life is going well
Yes 1 2 3 4 5 6 7 8 9 Don't pray

I try to meet with other Christians weekly
Yes 1 2 3 4 5 6 7 8 9 Never

I think that God is changing me slowly
Yes 1 2 3 4 5 6 7 8 9 No change

I let people know I'm a Christian
Yes 1 2 3 4 5 6 7 8 9 No one

I attend worship in church
Yes 1 2 3 4 5 6 7 8 9 Never

I receive Holy Communion
Yes 1 2 3 4 5 6 7 8 9 Never

I want to remain united with Jesus
Yes 1 2 3 4 5 6 7 8 9 No

27

If you could say yes to the last one that's where we all begin.
Ask God to help you in the other things, maybe you could meet with others to practice being united to Jesus together!

Lord, I need your help. I can't change myself. I want to remain united with you. Make me more like you Lord Jesus. Amen.

28

> 'I am the vine, and you are the branches. Whoever remains in me, and I in him, will bear much fruit; for you can do nothing without me.'
>
> John 15:5

We've pictured Jesus in lots of different ways over the last 27 units. We end with the key to our Christian life. Jesus said that he is the vine and we are the branches! A branch stays alive because it is attached to the trunk and part of the vine. Sap flows to the branch and because of that, fruit is made! You don't see many branches lying on the floor producing fruit. They have to stay part of the vine.

A Christian is someone who remains attached to Jesus. The Holy Spirit is the sap that flows into us. He produces fruit in us.

Read about the fruit that the Holy Spirit makes in us.

> But the Spirit produces love, joy, peace, patience, kindness, goodness, faithfulness, humility, and self-control. There is no law against such things as these.
>
> Galatians 5:22–23

When you read this list out. Who does it remind you of? Anybody you know? The answer is YES... Jesus. This list of fruit that the Holy Spirit grows in us is an exact picture of what Jesus is like. The Holy Spirit makes us more like Jesus in our daily lives.

Think of a practical situation where you might find the following fruit blossoming (for example, love—meeting your enemy and sensing God's love for them).

Love...

....

Joy..

....

Peace..

....

Patience....................................

....

Kindness...................................

....

Goodness..................................

....

Faithfulness..............................

....

Humility....................................

....

Self-control...............................

....

28

Heavenly Father, thank you for helping me to picture Jesus. I want to remain joined to him and have your Holy Spirit make me like him. Apart from Jesus I can do nothing. But with him all things are possible. Praise you Lord. Amen.

P.S. Jesus pictures himself as the vine which is all the branches together. Staying in the vine means being alongside all the other branches. Together we make up the vine. Together as the vine we show Jesus to the world.

Branching out!

29
What next?

The Following Jesus Series

If you have enjoyed using *Picturing Jesus*, you might like to look at other titles in the series.

Following Jesus presents a lively and stimulating introduction to the Christian faith in words and cartoons. Suitable for use as a confirmation course, the 31 steps/units (with practical suggestions and prayers) cover the basics of Christian teaching and discipleship. An additional leaflet is available which provides leaders with suggestions for four weekly sermons. Price: £2.99 per copy (£25 for a pack of 10).

Serving Jesus tackles many of the questions and problems facing young people as they try to serve Jesus. A further 27 units are presented, each linked with a character or event from the New Testament and including a short Bible reading and prayer. *Serving Jesus* will be particularly suitable for those who have just been confirmed. Price: £1.95 per copy (£15 for a pack of 10).

Praying with Jesus presents 28 units which each explore one aspect of 'praying with Jesus', with a Bible reading, comment and short assignment. *Praying with Jesus* will appeal to confirmation and post-confirmation candidates and any person anxious to learn more about prayer. Price £1.95 per copy (£15 for a pack of 10).

The Power of Jesus contains 28 units which consider the power of Jesus as seen in the seven signs in John's Gospel. Price: £2.99 per copy (£25 for a pack of 10).

Another 7 titles are planned in the *Following Jesus* series.

All titles in the series are illustrated throughout by Taffy.

Following Jesus, *Serving Jesus*, *Praying with Jesus* and *The Power of Jesus* are available now from all good Christian Bookshops, or in case of difficulty from BRF, Peter's Way, Sandy Lane West, Oxford, OX4 5HG. If ordering direct from BRF please add 15% (minimum 85p) to cover post and packing.

If you would like to know more about the full range of Bible reading notes and other Bible reading group study materials published by the Bible Reading Fellowship, write and ask for a free catalogue.

THE POWER OF JESUS

THE FOLLOWING JESUS SERIES

DO YOU THINK WE OUGHT TO WAKE HIM?

Nick Aiken
SERIES EDITOR: JAMES JONES
ILLUSTRATED BY

FOLLOWING JESUS

FIRST STEPS

James Jones
ILLUSTRATED BY TAFFY